the Princess in You

Foreword by
Dr. Tracy Quintana

KISHMA A. GEORGE, DANIELLE ASHLEY, LAKISHA SELBY,
MARLA SMITH, AYANNA LYNNAY, LAKESHA LOGAN,
ROMELLA VAUGHN, LETISHA GALLOWAY & TAMMY COLLINS MARKEE

The Princess in You

The Princess in YOU © April 2017

By K.A.G. (Kishma A. George Enterprises)

Published in the United States of America by
ChosenButterflyPublishing LLC

www.cb-publishing.com
Editing by Stephanie Montgomery, Unique Communications Concepts
Cover design CTS Graphic Designs

ISBN: 978-1-945377-00-6
First Edition Printing
Printed in the United States

Table of Contents

Foreword by Dr. Tracy Quintana.......

"The purpose in a man's heart is like deep water, but a man of understanding will draw it out." Proverbs 20:5 (ESV)

Hidden deep within your heart you will find that royalty resides in there. Longing, waiting and desiring to gush out like a mighty flowing river. You have been chosen, called out, set apart, marked, red flagged and destined for greatness. You are exquisite, finely detailed and designed. There is nothing too difficult for you; you have been fearfully and wonderfully made, by God Himself.

Though circumstances and situations may arise throughout our lives that seem to push down deep our God-Given-Destiny and hide the very royalty that we are. Making it impossible at times to clearly see, feel and know how glorious we have been created by the King to be. Until now!

This book, **The Princess in You,** is so amazing. Each Author has uniquely and brilliantly handed you over several keys to access your hidden potential. With step by step, simple and understandable ways to unveil, draw completely out and bring back into view, the true Princess in You. The world is going to know who you are! I highly recommend that you read this book, fix your crown, stand tall and let the floodgates of your royalty burst out, no holding back. The Princess in you is ready to arise!

Dr. Tracy Quintana, Co-founder of Embassy International Global Ministries; Pastor, City of the Lord Kingdom Training Center; Professor, Kingdom Government University, Pueblo, Co-Author, *I Prophesy Breakthrough*

www.embassyinternationalglobalministries.com

Learning Your True Identity!
by Ayanna Lynnay

Who are you? I know that seems like a weird question, but have you ever wondered who you really are and how you became that person? Many times, we don't realize who we are or the reason why we exist until we reach our 30's, 40's or older. Sadly, there are people who never discover their identity or who they were meant to be, so they go through life without a real sense of purpose. They live life each day until they get old and eventually die. When we don't know our purpose, we often find ourselves just existing - which makes us feel depressed and hopeless; it becomes easy to believe God doesn't have a plan or purpose for our life. I remember feeling that way. I seemed to have several things going for myself; a good job, family, and friends, but I found myself thinking *There has to be more to life than this!'*

Have you *ever* felt like that - like there was more to life than what you were experiencing? What if I said you don't have to wait until you're older; you can learn what your purpose in life is right now - would you want to know? Well that is what this chapter is about; learning your true identity!

It's important to know who you are in order to prevent people from negatively affecting your life. What do I mean? Well let's take bullying for example: bullies thrive off of calling people names, spreading lies or half-truths and intimidation.

When a person doesn't know who they are, it is easy for bullies to mentally break down the person they've targeted. Many times bullies are insecure and unhappy with their own identity and therefore try to make others insecure and unhappy as well. I'm sure you've heard the saying 'Misery loves company'; well it is true - miserable people create more miserable people and it's doubtful they realize what they are doing. They feel ugly, so they point out all of your flaws. Sometimes they even make up things just to make you feel bad about yourself.

It breaks my heart when I hear people accepting negative words from others; they store those words in their heart and believe them. Young girls who may have been told they were ugly, too fat or too skinny, etc. have altered their bodies drastically simply because they believed negative things people said. Some girls question their sexuality and expose themselves to relationships God never intended, simply because they aren't typical 'girly girls'. I've seen young ladies mistakenly go too far with guys - then people begin calling them names; before long, they stop defending themselves and act just like the names they've been called.

Think about this; if you are constantly being called a negative name, the first time you may say 'That's not true!' However, what if you were constantly hearing it from various people? If you aren't sure who you are, you may start to believe you are that name. This is why it's essential for you to learn who you are and to identify your purpose. Although the process of discovering your true identity and purpose can take years, if not a lifetime; you are able to know who you are NOT and that knowledge alone can prevent heartache and pain.

I can go on and on about this subject, but for the sake of time and space I'll share bullet points to start you on your journey of discovering your true identity.

1. **Your True Identity is Revealed by God.**

If you want to know how something works, ask the person who made it or read the owner's manual. The same goes for us. The Lord created us and He knows our purpose. There is a Scripture in the Bible where the Lord tells the prophet Jeremiah that before he (Jeremiah) was formed, the Lord already knew him and called him to be a prophet. In another Scripture, the Lord is telling Jeremiah that He knows the plans He has for Jeremiah and they are good. The Lord let Jeremiah know that he had to seek the Lord with his whole heart and when he did, he would find the Lord.

I believe the Lord is saying the same thing to each of us. He is saying _____ (insert your name) before you were formed in your mother's womb. I knew you. I called you to be a _____. I know the thoughts and plans that I have for you, plans to prosper you and not harm you, plans to give you hope and a future. _____ (insert your name) when you seek Me with your whole heart you will find Me.

How do you seek the Lord?

♛ **Pray:**   Prayer is a conversation with God. You start by simply talking to Him like you would a good friend. Before you finish, be quiet for a little while and see what He speaks to your heart.

♛ **Read the Bible:** Opening the Bible and just reading might not be easy for everyone. I suggest finding a Bible study book or a reading plan online. www.Biblegateway.com has free bible studies. You can also google Free Youth Bible Studies online. Say a prayer and ask the Lord to lead you to the one He wants you to start with.

♛ **Go to church:** The right church can really help you develop your relationship with the Lord. Ask the Lord to lead you to a church. Don't be surprised when people start inviting you to visit theirs. Go ahead and visit; He will speak to your heart when it is time to join.

♛ **Attend youth groups:** Youth groups can be a fun place where you can grow in your relationship with God because they are geared toward your age and issues you may be experiencing. Give youth groups a try!

👑 **Talk about Him with your friends:** As you learn about the Lord, share with your friends. You will find many are going through the same things you are and together you all can make it to the top with the Lord's help!

2. A Bad Beginning in Life Does Not Disqualify You from a Great Ending.

There are many people who experienced horrible childhoods, but eventually grew up and accomplished wonderful things in life. I once read that God allows His toughest soldiers to go through the biggest battles. Don't get me wrong, I am not saying God made bad things happen to you, but think about this - if two people shared their story about their high school graduations, whose story would you find most inspiring: Person A, who lived with both parents in a nice home and never experienced hard times - or Person B, who was raised in multiple foster homes, attended different high schools and often wanted to quit, but promised herself she would graduate high school and attend college no matter what? While both stories are inspiring, I am sure you'd agree that you'd wipe tears from your eyes after hearing Person B's story and witnessing her walking across the stage to receive her diploma.

The key is to see yourself successful and blessed, regardless how things may seem. Whether you're struggling in school or struggling in other areas of your life; picture yourself overcoming those struggles. You must change the way you view things. Instead of feeling inferior because of your challenges; envision success and think about how many people you will inspire when your situation changes - and believe me, it will eventually change.

3. Knowing Who You Are NOT Can Help Identify Who You Are.

As you grow into the beautiful woman God intends, decide to never accept any title or label God did not give you. For instance, you may have lied about something and were called a liar, but don't assume that label and keep lying. You may have stolen, but don't shrug your shoulders and say *'Oh well, I might as well keep stealing because everyone thinks I'm a thief anyway'*. Everyone makes mistakes and bad choices in life but never allow those mistakes and bad choices to label you. Instead - own up to them, apologize and try to do better.

4. Speak Great Things Over Your Own Life.

Words have power, which is why you must never speak negative words over your life or allow negative words from others to enter your heart. Speak good things over your life every time you hear someone (no matter who it is) say something negative about you. Speak good things over your life when negative thoughts enter your mind. Sometimes we can't help when negative thoughts occur, but we do have control over how long they remain. One way of removing those negative thoughts is by replacing them with positive, uplifting words. Every day, practice saying something positive about yourself and watch how those words will begin to shape your life!

As you read this book, it is my prayer you discover how special you are. Even if your parents did not plan you - you are no accident to God! The Lord created you with a special purpose and He has great plans for your life. No matter what you go through in life and no matter how bad things may seem, remember that you are a princess: You are the King's Daughter!

About Ayanna

Ayanna is a wife, mother, nurse, author, book publisher, mentor, minister and more. She loves the Lord and loves helping others grow in their relationship with the Lord.

You can connect with Ayanna via Facebook at https://www.facebook.com/TheTransformationStation/

Or by visiting www.cb-publishing.com

Ayanna's Acknowledgements

I thank the Lord for who He is in my life. He continues to bless me, despite myself and I am eternally grateful. Words could never express how happy and thankful I am that the Lord revealed some of the awesome plans He has for my life. My beginning looks nothing like my ending!

Thank you and I love you to; my husband, **Pastor Lawrence Moore Jr.** My beautiful daughters who are 18 years apart – Princess **Shakiya** & Princess **Lauriyana.** My bonus daughters Princess **Lauren**, Princess **Shekinah,** & Princess **Amya.** My mom **Margaret** and my sisters **Sonya** and **Melody.** My beautiful nieces Princess **Raven**, Princess **Tayla**, Princess **Micah**, Princess **Kylah** and my handsome nephews Prince **Aiden** and Prince **Jaxson**

Special thank you to; **Dr. Kishma** for being such a visionary and for constantly trusting me with delivering your babies (your books) and to my Editor extraordinaire – **Stephanie,** who I thank God for connecting us. I am so looking forward to trying our hand with fiction!

Finally, to **my sistas in Christ** who inspire me to be all I can be; **Pastor Rebecca, Pastor Joanna, Apostle Gloria, Pastor Shirley, Michelle T., Dishan, Prophetess Tanya H, Apostle Yolanda, Evangelist Karen, Evangelist Pat,** my **FaceBook Family** and **so many more...**

Find Your Purpose Within You!

by LaKesha C. Logan

Dear Princess,

Please know this above all things; there is a very unique purpose within you! You may have yet to discover exactly what this means - but in the process of learning yourself, know that you are not alone. Those closest to you - such as your parents, family members, friends, and mentors; love, support and are rooting for you! WE are all here to assist you in discovering your purpose every step of the way! You may not understand this right now, but just remember to embrace who you are, what makes you unique and all of the amazing things you are going to achieve once you Find Your Purpose Within You!

"You Are Fearfully and Wonderfully Made" (PS.139:14)

Love,

Ms. LaKesha C. Logan

Every Princess has a purpose! As you move through life, you will understand just how important it is to know the meaning of the word *Purpose*, what your purpose is on earth and the key role your purpose will play in everything you do. Let's briefly explore the meaning and importance of purpose and most of all - what it means to you.

What is 'Purpose'?
(Merriam-Webster Dictionary)

- *noun* pur·pose \ˈpər-pəs\   (Short Definition)
the reason why something is done or used : the aim or intention of something

: the feeling of being determined to do or achieve something

: the aim or goal of a person: what a person is trying to do, become, etc.

The Importance of Knowing Your Purpose

It is important to know your purpose because it is the essence of who you are and the impact you have upon the lives you touch and the world around you. Your purpose makes you both special and unique, so as you navigate through life - you should know how essential it is for you to operate in your purpose!

Discovering and walking in your purpose will help you:

- Become a woman of great character and integrity
- Become confident in who you are
- Be clear in what you were born to do
- Make smart choices regarding your dreams and aspirations
- Inspire others in the world around you
- Live a life of abundance, fulfillment and meaning

Now that you have a better understanding of the definition of 'Purpose' according to the Merriam Webster Dictionary, let's explore what purpose means to you. You can work on this basic exercise independently, with friends or a mentoring group, etc.

Below you will find the word PURPOSE broken down into separate letters. For each letter, write another word that is still representative of the word purpose. For example, 'P' could stand for Promise. If you choose to do this as a group exercise, be sure to share and discuss. You'll be surprised by how much you can inspire and learn from one another.

P_____

U_____

R_____

P_____

O_____

S_____

E_____

Embracing Your Purpose

Princess, now it's time to really embrace who you are and walk in it. This is the most amazing part of your journey; learning and appreciating all the attributes which make you different and special. Once you begin to walk in who you are, you will become unstoppable! This is where you truly begin to mature and understand that every experience you will ever have prepares you for your own greatness and purpose within. I am excited for you and honored to be a part of your journey!

Now listen, there will undoubtedly be times in your life when you'll compare yourself to others. Sometimes this is simply due to the fact that you are still learning who you are. Other times it stems from personal insecurities, or perhaps you never knew the meaning of purpose - or that you have a purpose of your own. Believe it or not - this curiosity, these emotions and questioning of 'self' is normal. Every girl and woman has or will travel down this exact same road sooner or later in life. Whatever you do, don't beat yourself up. When you find yourself feeling afraid, confused, unsure or doubting who you are and your abilities - remember these things:

- Always love and appreciate yourself no matter what.
- You are never alone; talk to those who care about and support you.
- There will only be ONE AMAZING YOU - There are no comparisons!

So, until you are clear on your purpose in life; stay true to yourself, lean on those who care for you and dare to be the absolute best expression of who you are! If you love to write,

write your own story. If you love to sing, create your own songs - and if you love to dance, dance to the rhythm and beat of your own drum. Do what you love that is creative and positive until you discover the very path which leads you to the purpose within!

Exploring Purpose and What it Means to You

Now that you know more about embracing your purpose, I want you to further explore with the following exercise. Again, feel free to share this exercise as a group and discuss. You never know what you might learn or share ☺

In your own words, what does 'Purpose' mean to you?

_____

_____

_____

_____

_____

_____

Do you know your purpose or at least have an idea? (If yes, please share and if no, simply list 1-2 things you really love to do and why).

_____

_____

_____

_____

_____

_____

👑 How do you see yourself operating in your purpose throughout the world?

_____

_____

_____

_____

_____

_____

_____

👑 How will your purpose impact the world around you? (Ex: Mentoring other girls/women, volunteering in a Senior Citizen Center, starting a movement to empower your community, running for president, etc.

_____

_____

_____

_____

_____

You Are Not Alone

Before I conclude, one of the most important golden nuggets of advice I can leave with my Princesses is this; **You Are Not Alone!** As you were reading, you may have asked yourself, "Why does she continue repeating this particular phrase?" I do so because I strongly feel that you need to know how powerful this truth really is. As girls and young women, it is imperative to know you do not have to walk this journey alone.

Perhaps you already have a circle of females (mothers, sisters, friends, mentors). But if not, don't fear. As you continue to grow in your purpose, destiny will surround you with other Princesses and Queens ready to embrace you right where you are, just as you are and everything you aspire to be! Life will not always be easy, but far less difficult once you're surrounded by a sisterhood.

So I'll say this once again, You Are Not Alone! Continue to believe in yourself and be determined to find your purpose within!

Love You Abundantly...

Princess Jordynn, Age 12
PA

"From my perspective, purpose is the reasoning of an action or word. My purpose is to bring forth positive change to the world through The Arts (acting, music and writing), achieving my goal and encouraging and inspiring others."

Princess Jordynn is active in the choir and in plays at her school.

Princess Lamajay, Age 15
Delaware

"Purpose for me means reaching a goal you set out to achieve. I believe my purpose is to be successful in mentoring others. I plan to walk in my purpose by dedicating time to helping people to be and do better. I want to help them discover and be interested in their own purpose too!"

Princess Lamajay enjoys doing hair, singing and is involved with The Communities in School Mentoring Program for teen girls and boys.

About LaKesha

LaKesha Chermelle Loga (L.C. Logan)

Ms. Logan has been a native of Chester, PA for over 35 years. She is the daughter of both the late Joseph James Logan Sr. and Jacqueline Juanita Genwright-Logan, the eldest of 3 siblings, and the proud mother of one son, Zion E. Logan. Ms. Logan attended the Chester Upland School District, and graduated from Chester High School in 1992.

Several years later, Ms. Logan became a single mother of one son Zion E. Logan. It was then she truly realized that she needed to make some major life changes. Therefore, she resigned from a corporate entity to work for a local nonprofit.

This opportunity allowed her the flexibility to enroll in college for the very first time. In doing so, Ms. Logan attended and graduated from the I-LEAD program through Harcum College. She became the 1st generation college graduate in her immediate family, with an Associates Degree of Science in Organizational Leadership.

In 2009, Ms. Logan envisioned and manifested her own empowerment group for women, which would later be known as the Phenomenal Women's Network (PWN). PWN focuses on the empowerment of women from all walks of life. In doing so, PWN continues to impact through not only the empowerment of women, but girls, families, and communities.

In many ways, Ms. Logan is a testament of tragedy to triumph. If asked, she will tell you that her life is full and rich which gifts, blessings, and opportunities that in some cases, she would have never imagined. She recently resigned from her career and position as Head of Youth Services after 11 years to pursue her passion in building PWN and continued efforts to empower & impact the lives of others.

Last but not least, Ms. Logan is now a Co-Author of **The Princess in You** book project along with a group of amazing female authors, leaders, and trailblazers. She is looking forward to authoring her own independent book project as well as future collaborations and partnerships. Ms. Logan understands that it takes hard work, sweat, and sometimes tears in birthing greatness and bringing forth positive change. She knows the importance of her purpose and is committed to continuing to be a pillar of inspiration, love, and strength in the world around her.

LaKesha's Acknowledgments

First I must thank God, The Creator of all that is good and perfect. God - not knowing any better, I searched everywhere, yet I found there is none like You. My heart will praise You forever and ever!

Secondly, I would be remiss if I didn't acknowledge and honor both my Father and Mother. To the late Joseph James Logan Sr.; for not only giving me life - but also your happy eyes, sense of humor, wit, and foundation of love as a little girl. I still remember you placing me on your shoulders and us walking to the store for ice cream. I always felt safe and strong. I will forever remember our memories, I love you Daddy Joe.

To the years of love, struggle and triumph with my great Queen Mother, Jacqueline Juanita Genwright Logan; I believe you also were always the wind beneath my wings and my greatest fan. Oh how my heart so longs for you to be here with me. My eyes fill with mixed emotion of tears even as I write this, but I know somehow that you are proud of me as you have always been. As I've always said; 'Mom, I am an extension and nothing without you...I still say that I would have never been anything without you'. Thanks for all of the seeds planted...If you can see me, sit back and watch them grow, watch the fruit of your labor manifest and know that together you & God did it girl! Until we meet again, I love you Mama J.

Thanks to my beautiful son Zion E. Logan. You are both my greatest gift and biggest supporter! From the time you were a little boy to now as a young man, you've always been able to see beyond my flaws, love me unconditionally as your Mother, share me as an Earth Mother to so many other children and young adults - and still believe in me for whatever I put my mind, energy and hands to as an Artist, Visionary and now Co-Author! We've always and will forever be a team! Thanks for being a blessing and a wonderful son. I could not have possibly asked God for more!

Thanks Mr. Keith S. Andrews, for not only being a friend - but also often as a silent partner, wind beneath my wings, push when I need a shove and confidant.

To Ms. Kishma George, you are simply amazing! You are an awesome woman of God, purpose and vision. Thanks beyond words for involving me in this beautiful project! Words cannot express my gratitude, especially during such a remarkable season of reaping what we've sown. This opportunity has not only been a true honor, but an instrument of healing and birthing for me through writing. May God continue to bless you and shine through your life!

Special thanks to one of my most recent precious gifts and sister connections, Artist Marcy Morris. God couldn't have connected us any more perfectly! Oh, by the way everyone - Marcy makes the best all-natural product cookies ever☺ Please check out: http://diversitycookies.com/. The best healthy cookies ever with a meaning behind them!

Lastly, I want to send special thanks to Princess Jordynn, Princess Lamajay - every Princess I've ever worked with and those whom I have yet to meet. It is because of YOU that Queens like me do what we do. We love you and will continue to fight for your destiny and purpose because you are worthy of finding, embracing and walking in your purpose!

DESTINY

by Romella Vaughn

"Commit thy works unto the Lord, and thy thoughts shall be established," Proverbs 16:3 (KJV).

FINDING PURPOSE

When God created each and every one of us, He had a plan and purpose for our lives. Knowing and walking in your purpose is very important. Of course, as teenagers, wanting to know our purpose is the last thing on our minds. As teenagers, we want to keep up with the latest fashions and hairstyles, wear makeup, go to dances and games, talk on our cell phones, etc. Is it fun? Of course, it is! But, that's not what life is always about. Life is about helping others; it's not always about us. There are so many people in need and God wants to use you.

In my teen years, I didn't have anyone to explain the meaning of purpose and why is it so important. As for you, I want to help you discover your purpose. What's purpose? Purpose: *The object toward which one strives or for which something exists; an aim or goal.* Walking in purpose changes the hard times into valuable resources which give you wisdom and inspiration to fulfill your purpose. It also helps you understand why you went through what you experienced. How do you discover your purpose? If you're ready to walk in purpose, pray and ask God 'What's my purpose?' Also, ask Him for guidance and assistance.

When God speaks, you must move and complete the task set before you. Delayed obedience is disobedience. Remember that you have to take destiny steps; everything won't be given to you all at once. Your footsteps are ordered by the Lord! Having the Lord in your life makes things so much better!

At 41 years of age, I decided to ask God "What's my purpose?" Yes, 41 years old! Did I get an answer right away? No! It was months later when God instructed me to write my first book *Naked*, which is part of my purpose. When we think God isn't listening, He's listening.

YOUR STRUGGLES ARE PART OF YOUR PURPOSE

"*Cast not away therefore your confidence, which hath great recompense of reward. For ye have need of patience, that, after ye have done the will of God, ye might receive the promise,*" Hebrews 10:35-36 (KJV).

Do you know that God will use the very same thing which haunts you - has you up late at night and makes you want to give up, in order to help others? The process is necessary. We have to experience trials and tribulations so that they strengthen us, make us tough and prepare us for our DESTINY. Destiny is where God wants to take us. Whatever you do - don't make a permanent decision based on a temporary situation. Just know that God is with you the entire time. It doesn't matter if you didn't complete high school, have a college degree and/or believe you aren't smart enough: you can do all things through Christ Jesus. Remember, out of small places comes big things. Understand your value and worth! You are unique in your own way. God wants to take you from the back of the line, to the front of the line!

Throughout my life, I knew there was a book inside of me but I didn't think I was smart enough to write one. Well, with only a high school diploma - I've completed my first book within two months. You can do anything you set your mind to do. It takes time, sacrifice and effort to accomplish your goal. God wants you to take the initiative; He will help and guide you through and most of all - He will finish it for you. It's not for you to worry about the help and the resources; God will connect all the dots. It's already done! Always surround yourself with people who make positive deposits into your life, not just withdrawals. No matter what you do, DON'T GIVE UP! God is ready to propel you towards your destiny!

WALKING IN PURPOSE:

<u>P</u>: **Persistence:** the quality that allows someone to continue doing something or trying to do something, even though it is difficult or opposed by other people

<u>U</u>: **Unique:** very special or unusual

<u>R</u>: **Radiant:** bright and shining

<u>P</u>: **Princess:** a woman having sovereign power

<u>O</u>: **Omnipotent:** having unlimited power; able to do anything.

<u>S</u>: **Strong:** able to withstand great force or pressure

<u>E</u>: **Excellence:** the quality of being outstanding or extremely good

ARE YOU READY TO WALK IN PURPOSE AND GET TO YOUR DESTINATION? FASTEN YOUR SEATBELT AND GET READY FOR TAKE OFF!

DESTINY STEPS

D~ DREAM BIG: You are destined for greatness. It's time to make your dream a reality. Are you ready to write your visions and dreams? *"And the LORD answered me, and said, Write the vision, and make it plain upon tables, that he may run that readeth it,"* **Habakkuk 2:2 (KJV).**

Pray and wait on instructions from God. Have **FAITH** and trust God while waiting! Be patient! Delay doesn't equal denial.
What are the goals you want to achieve? What's your passion? Don't forget to DREAM BIG!

_____

_____

_____

_____

_____

_____

_____

E~EFFORT: Putting forth effort isn't always easy because of distractions in our lives, but it is important. If you don't put effort into your dreams and do what's required of you - nothing will get done and before you know it, life will pass you by.

I want to challenge you! List the things you WILL accomplish within the next six months.

Ex: I'm making a commitment to feed the homeless every 1st and 3rd Saturday, starting next weekend.

_____

_____

_____

_____

_____

_____

_____

_____

_____

_____

_____

S~ STRIVE: *to achieve or obtain something; to struggle or fight forcefully.*

Whatever you do, DON'T GIVE UP! Fight for what you want. The enemy tells you that you can't and places obstacles in your path, but God created you to be a fighter. Think back to the obstacles which were thrown before you. Didn't you survive? You can do it!

Write down a storm that was so challenging, you never thought you would make it. When you are having doubts and want to give up, revert back to this storm so that it encourages you and helps you to persevere.

_____

_____

_____

_____

_____

_____

_____

_____

_____

_____

_____

_____

T~ TENACITY: *the quality or fact of being able to grip something firmly*
No matter how the situation looks and how hard it gets, keep pushing. Despite what people say about you, keep pushing. No matter who walks out of your life, keep pushing. Hold fast to your dream!

I~ INITIATE: *to begin, set going, or originate.*

God is waiting for us to make the first move; He gives us free will. He is waiting on you to ask, *"What's my purpose?"* God promotes based on our heart, not our head. He is looking for Himself in you. Are you ready?

Below, write down the time and date when you ask God *"What's my purpose?"*

_____

_____

_____

_____

_____

_____

_____

_____

N~ NO: No isn't an option when God gives you an assignment. There will be times when God asks us to do something which won't make sense, or it might be something we don't want to do, but it must be done. NEVER say NO to God. That very same thing you don't want to do is connected to where God wants to take you. It will eventually lead to your destiny.

Y~ YES: Always say YES when God asks you to do something, even when it doesn't make sense! When you decide to say YES, your life will change. God will begin removing people from your life who are toxic and serve as distractions. Avoid negativity and distractions. You must bring change to your life! God requires us to spend more time with Him so that He can pour ideas and strategies into us. God is ready to give you your first assignment. Are you ready? Have faith and trust God, even when you can't trace Him. Praise and thank God for what He's about to do in your life! God loves you so much! *"For God so loved the world, that He gave His only begotten Son, that whosoever believeth in Him should not perish, but have everlasting life" John 3:16 (KJV)*

YOU HAVE REACHED YOUR DESTINATION!

About Romella

Evangelist Romella Holmes Vaughn is a crusader. She was an ambitious and precocious young girl, born in New Orleans in 1972 to Randy Holmes and Patsy Kador. Growing up, she watched her mother struggle with alcohol and drug abuse, which rendered her incapable of raising Vaughn and her three siblings. As a child, she had a natural curiosity about life. While growing up feeling hopeless, bitter and lonely; not wanting to live anymore, she had no idea it was a set up for the wonderful life God has now blessed her with. As an adult, her concerns about the nationwide, high rate of teen suicide and other life-threatening social issues grew; this was God's instruction to write her first book *Naked*.

Naked paints a portrait of the intense, mind boggling struggles an individual can experience without anyone knowing. The purpose of the book is to convey a message of hope to those who are struggling with mental issues, suicidal thoughts, depression, anxiety, unforgiveness, drug and alcohol addiction, hopelessness and despair. *Naked* was written to expose and offer prayer solutions to the darkness which endeavors to overtake us.

Vaughn is also the Co-Author of *Dreaming the Dream* and now **The Princess in You**!

Endeavoring to continue fighting the good fight of faith to help others; this play exposes other social ills that are so prevalent, yet invisible in our society. Vaughn continues to wait on instructions from God.

Romella's Acknowledgements

To my **Heavenly Father**, thank You so much for Your precious son, Jesus! Jesus, thank You for everything You have done for us! God, it was You who protected me throughout my journey; ordered my footsteps, was there when I needed a shoulder to cry on and provided for me. You proved I can do anything put before me. You looked past all my flaws and loved me unconditionally, which means a lot to me. Thank You so much for Your Grace and Mercy and the gifts You have blessed me with. Thanks for trusting me with Your people! You are AWESOME AND AMAZING! I LOVE YOU!

To **Jude, my husband, best friend and confidante**; for the love you have shown me over the years and supporting every decision I've made. When I'm down, you're always there to pick me up. You have been an amazing father to our children; I thank God for placing you in our lives! Thank you for being patient with me during the process of writing, I love you and always will!

In memory of **my beloved mother, Patsy Kador**: I love and miss you dearly.

To **Randy Holmes SR.**, for being the best dad in the world! In spite of everything you went through, you did what you could to protect and provide for your four kids whom you raised on your own. I love you!

To **Bishop T.D. Jakes**, for allowing God to use you to help His people. Words cannot express my gratitude to you for being an awesome Pastor and Teacher. God placed me under your ministry in 2014, which is one of the best things to ever happen to me. You helped me complete my very first book *Naked*. Thank you so much for your tenacity and your wonderful teaching!

To **Kentrell, Bria and Lil Jude** - my children, for being the loves of my life. There's not a day that goes by when I don't think about you. I love you with all of my heart. Remember, you can do anything you set your mind to. Always keep God in your lives and allow Him to direct your paths!

To **Dr. Kishma George**; for allowing me the opportunity to co-author this book project, for believing in me and for being obedient. When I decided to bring change into my life, I prayed for God to place people in my life who would motivate me, teach me, believe in me and who are God-fearing; that's you! Thank you so much for being who you are and for opening your heart to help others. God bless you and I love you!

Contact Author Romella Vaughn

Website: www.authorromellav.com
Facebook: <u>Romella Vaughn</u>
Instagram: _authorromellav
Twitter: @authorromellav
authorrvaughn@gmail.com

Against All Odds
by Letisha Galloway

When the odds are stacked against you, getting to your 'happily ever after' may seem impossible. It isn't impossible. Within the word impossible, is the word 'possible'. In this life anything is possible. Coming against all the negativity in the world is not an easy task, but it is possible. The world is full of more negativity than positivity - but you have the power to change what surrounds you. The world is full of media images which show how we are supposed to look and act; those images are not always correct. We should keep a clean appearance. We do not have to wear expensive clothing in order to look good. Knowing the difference is important.

In life it's not easy to feel uncomfortable. No one wants to feel uncomfortable. It is natural to desire a life which is smooth and without any bumps on the road leading to what you wish to accomplish. At times, there will be discomfort in areas of life requiring growth. When you take time to see you have potential and options for your life - you will realize there are more opportunities for victory.

What you think, has a connection to what you feel and how you act. If you think you will never be successful - you will feel and act in a way which shows that you don't believe in yourself. Others can tell when you don't believe in yourself and may take advantage. Having confidence on the inside will show on the outside; a lack of confidence shows on the outside as well. At times, our outward appearance looks fine to others; we are smiling, but deep down we have a fear of something.

Everyone has something they are afraid to do or become. Fear keeps us from reaching our full potential. The problem with fear is that it robs us of our destiny and may prevent you from trying things. For some - there is a fear of failure. The issue with fearing failure is that you don't know what will happen until you try. If what you tried doesn't work the first time, try again. Many people throughout history failed before they achieved success. Walt Disney failed at first, however today Disney makes billions from merchandise, movies, theme parks and cruises. It wasn't easy for him to achieve success. Walt Disney had his own rough start and was fired from a job because 'he lacked imagination and good ideas'. After he was fired, Walt Disney started a number of businesses which didn't last long and ended in bankruptcy and failure – but he never gave up. If Walt Disney had given up, the world would have never experienced or enjoyed anything Disney-related.

Thomas Edison was told he could never learn anything and was fired from his first two jobs for not being productive. Even as an inventor, Edison made 1,000 unsuccessful attempts trying to invent the light bulb. He never gave up, nor listened to the people who doubted his ability. He didn't let what his teachers said to him as a child, prevent him from doing what others called impossible. If Mr. Edison had quit, we would still be in the dark after the sun goes down.

Oprah Winfrey experienced failure before she reached success. Oprah is known as one of the most famous faces to ever appear on television. She is also known as one of the richest and most successful women in the world, however becoming successful was not easy for Oprah. She survived an abusive childhood and had many career setbacks - including being fired from her job as a television reporter. Despite many odds against her, Oprah decided she would keep going. Had she decided to quit, the world would have never experienced The Oprah Winfrey Show. Her show helped a lot of people on a global scale. Oprah's show ended, but people can still watch reruns. Involved in many outreach efforts across the world; Oprah provided a great deal of help to the continent of Africa by providing a place for girls to become educated. These are places where girls can defy the odds much like Oprah has.

Walt Disney, Thomas Edison and Oprah Winfrey all have similar things in common; they didn't let the odds stop them. They each experienced failure before reaching success. During the process, I am sure they became discouraged - but they kept going, fear may be present, but don't let it take over your life. Even if you're not as successful as you wish, you must keep going. Someone in the world needs what you can offer. If you stop, people will never benefit from what you know or create.

Having a positive mindset is crucial to overcome challenges. When someone says that you cannot do something, you have a choice to make. The choice is not easy; it is often made difficult from hearing negative things and your surroundings. You must decide to adopt a positive outlook on life. No one can change your thinking, but you. You have the power to change your thoughts. You can change your thoughts from 'I can't' to 'I can'; from 'I won't' to 'I will' and from 'no' to 'yes'. Believe you can go after what you want in life. You will be successful and yes, you will continue to try. Positive thinking sets you up for great success. It all starts in your mind. When you've been speaking negative words to yourself, it may take a while to get used to speaking good things into your life. Each day make it a habit to tell yourself something good about yourself. Tell yourself things such as, 'I am beautiful and worthy of great things in life'. Say that today is going to be a great day. Starting your morning each day with positive self-talk enables you to have a great start. If you speak negative words about yourself or your day, you've already defeated the purpose by using your own words against you. Speak life!

In this world people are quick to label others. Some labels are encouraging, while others are discouraging. When I was 10 months old, my legs were removed. Because of my physical disability, I was labeled early on. My great-grandmother was told that I would be better off in a school with children like me. When this story was shared with me later in life, I didn't understand why the teachers would make such a statement; they labeled me before I even started school. They already decided that based on my physical disability, I shouldn't be placed in public school. I was in private school, then placed in public school in the third grade because I had a learning disability; I wasn't given a chance. By 5th grade I was in all special education classes, except gym. I didn't understand why

I was there. I couldn't understand why the teachers and administrators didn't take the time to see that I didn't need special education classes.

I became saddened, disappointed and started to give up on myself. I started to tell myself I would never be in the same classes as the other children. Every child I knew wasn't in special education classes all day, but I was. I felt singled out and embarrassed. I believed I would never be what I wanted when I grew up. I told myself negative things every day. With each passing day, my hope seemed further and further away. I didn't understand that I was discouraging myself, along with others. I was giving their words credit by supporting them with my own negativity.

In class I talked a lot. The teachers would 'shush me' and tell me to be quiet. Once day, a teacher asked me why I was talking and I said I was bored. I said, "I always finish my work and I'm bored". She didn't know what else to say, so she returned to her desk. She called my great-grandmother and we all met with school administrators. Like previously, they said I belonged in all special education classes and they brought worksheets and activities for me to complete. My great-grandmother and teacher believed I could do the work and encouraged me. I passed activity after activity and worksheet after worksheet. After that meeting, it was agreed I would be moved into all mainstream classes, except for math. It takes believing in yourself - not taking 'no' for an answer, to get where you want or need to be. Later, I proceeded to write books and graduate from college. A guidance counselor once said I wasn't college material; not only was I college material, I was graduate school material. It can be done. Nothing in life will be perfect - we all make mistakes along the way. It would be nice to say that I achieved all of these wonderful things and didn't have obstacles along the way towards earning my degrees, but I can't say that. I made mistakes along the way.

After high school I took an admissions test for college. The tests are designed to assess if students require classes before their main courses of study. I tested and was very disappointed. In high school I made honor roll 10th through 12th grades. I felt as though it was happening all over again; I was told I had to take a math class which I expected - but I was very discouraged when I was informed I had to take a reading comprehension test as well. I took the classes because I had to complete those classes before I could register. I entered community college with two scholarships and financial aid. I had two other classes to take before I could register for college-level math.

I was comfortable in college and did well my first semester. The next semester however, I started neglecting my assignments. I would often say I would complete them later; later arrived when I almost failed my classes, but by then it was too late. I was unable to recover from not doing what I was supposed to do. I was warned twice by the Dean of Students and other faculty that I was close to being suspended from financial aid, but I didn't take the situation seriously. I didn't pay attention to what was happening. I repeated this cycle until I was advised I couldn't receive any more financial aid. The end of financial aid meant the end of my college career - or so I thought. Sometimes the mistakes we make cause us to change direction.

When I moved from New Jersey to Delaware, I wasn't sure if I could return to college but the financial aid representative said I could start over on financial aid. I don't think she understood the impact those words had on me at that moment; I came in very discouraged, yet left with hope. It doesn't hurt to smile or say an encouraging word to someone much like she did. After being admitted, I was sent to Student Support Services where there were guidance counselors for students who were first to graduate college in their immediate family. I received a lot of encouragement and we discussed what I should do differently this time. I accepted responsibility for not trying as hard as I should have previously.

At this community college; I attended every class, completed all of my assignments and paid attention to important things. One of my instructors said after class that I must have always been a good student. I shared that I failed at my previous institution and she couldn't believe it. I learned from and owned my past mistakes. I decided this time would be different. I learned what the consequences were from not completing assignments; I learned from everything I experienced and used it to knock down the odds of me not graduating from college at all.

What you wish to achieve can appear far away, just like the side mirror of a car says 'objects are closer than they appear'. Your victory is closer than it appears. You have the power to decide whether you will face your obstacles or let them overpower you. With prayer and determination, anything is possible. Only you can decide to climb over or walk around your obstacles. Only you can decide to succeed against all odds. Life can be challenging, but don't make it more challenging by not believing in yourself and your abilities. You have the ability to achieve great things. You will achieve great things in this life. I believe in you. Now go out into the world and show them what you can really do.

<u>Speak to yourself</u>

This activity encourages you to speak positive things each morning. It is important to encourage yourself before facing the world each day. At the end, take time to complete the 'I am' statements.

I can do it

I can be successful

I love myself

I am a good person

I am beautiful

I am smart

I am a great friend

I can make a difference in the world

It will be a great day

My future is greater than my present

Now you complete the following statements!

I am_____

I am_____

I am_____

I am_____

I am_____

I am_____

I am_____

I am_____

I am_____

I am_____

I am_____

I am_____

I am_____

I am_____

About Letisha

Letisha Galloway is from Woodstown, New Jersey and currently resides in Delaware. Letisha is an author signed to Imani Faith Publishing, inspirational speaker and poet. She obtained a Master of Science degree in Administration of Human Service and a Master of Science degree in Administration of Justice from Wilmington University. Letisha is presently a Senior Social Worker/Case Manager in Delaware.

Letisha empowers people to follow their God-given destiny. Through her various social media accounts and blogs, she frequently empowers people to leave their comfort zones to chase their destiny. She believes that everyone has a purpose and that when a person discovers what they love to do, they have found their purpose.

Letisha is regularly involved with bringing awareness to domestic violence and child abuse. As a domestic violence survivor, Letisha is a strong advocate for change and protection for those who feel they have no voice. Additionally, she advocates for ending hunger and homelessness. Letisha is the mother of a son, Jordan who is resting peacefully in the arms of God.

She may be contacted through her website www.letishagalloway.com

Email: letisha.nicole@gmail.com

and Facebook:

https://www.facebook.com/authorletishagalloway

Letisha's Acknowledgements

First, I would like to thank God for leading me through this awesome journey. HE never gave up on me and for that I am eternally grateful. I want to thank my angels in heaven; my great-grandmother Genevieve (Mom), my sister Kristen, my son Jordan and the other loved ones who have gone to be with the Lord. Thank you to Cheryl Lacey Donovan for helping me realize my dreams and for believing in me.

Thank you to Elissa Gabrielle and Peace in the Storm Publishing for believing in me. Thank you to my mother. Thank you to my father, stepmother and brother for your encouragement. Thank you to my aunts; Sandra, Gina and Net for your love and support. Thank you to my Grammy Mary for your support and continued prayers. Thank you to my Uncle Larry who pushed me to reach a little higher in life and believed in me when very few did. To my Aunt Cecelia - thanks for your kind words and encouragement. Thank you to my sister Kym who I can always count on for a laugh and encouragement.

Thank you to my Uncle, Pastor C.V. Holmes. Thank you to my friends who support me; Lydia, Angel, Shanda, Michelle, Hurley and many others. Thank you to my friend and visionary of this project, Dr. Kishma George. Thank you to my nieces and nephews; Jamyla, Lailoni, James and Jaleel

(Elijah is on the way) - who I can always count on to make me laugh and brighten my day. Auntie loves you, more than you will ever know. Thank you to all of my grandparents for their love and kindness. Thank you to all of my family who have shown their love and support - there are too many of you to name. Thank you to Apostle Faye Richardson, Bishop Donald Richardson and the Bread of Life Christian Church family for their love and kindness. Thank you to anyone who has ever supported my dreams and encouraged me. Thank you to those of you who have purchased this book; may God continue to bless you and lift you higher.

Building Your Confidence
Mirror, Mirror, What do I See?

by Lakisha Selby

Life as a young lady can be very difficult, overwhelming and stressful at times. Today, young girls are feeling the pressure of trying to find their identity and fit into this world with many expectations. This chapter of the *Princess in You* is designed to help young ladies build their confidence and become all that God has created them to be in their community, home and school. Your confidence will not develop overnight - it will take practice. There are areas where you feel more confident than others.

Before you begin this chapter, think about the areas in your life where you lack confidence. Write them down on the lines provided to help you reflect while reading this chapter:

1. _____

2. _____

3. _____

4. _____

5. _____

6. _____

7. _____

8. _____

9. _____

10. _____

Now that you've had the chance to think about those areas in your life where you lack confidence, let's take a ride down confidence lane for ten days.

Our first stop will be on *I Am Beautiful Block*. Look in the mirror and what do you see? If the mirror is not clean - you will see yourself as fat, skinny, ugly, wishing for long or short hair, thinking of being someone else or believing lies that you were not pretty enough. Embrace the beautiful young lady looking into the mirror and remember you were not created to look like anyone else in the world. You are beautiful just the way you are.

It's time to clean the mirror and repeat these words; I AM BEAUTIFUL and make sure you have a smile on your face. You are not what your family, peers or media portray you to be. You are a beautiful princess.

Let's move to our next stop on *I Am Good Enough Block*. Stop being so hard on yourself; no one is perfect. I know you are under a lot of pressure to be the best you can be. You have to be the best daughter, friend, sister, student, role model, etc. It's time to be honest with yourself and realize you can't be everything to everyone - however, you can be everything to you. Don't compare yourself to other young ladies You Are Good Enough!

Let's continue to drive down the blocks - don't get tired just yet. When you arrive at *I Am Worth It Block*, make a right - pull over and park. As a young lady, you must know your worth. You don't have to settle for less; remember you deserve so much more. Often times young girls who don't have a father in their life or who had a father - but was not shown love in the home, will seek boys for attention. Frequently, young girls are just looking for someone to love or just to hear the words 'I Love You'. Don't get desperate for love; love will come to you and you must learn how to love yourself first.

You deserve more than the boy who talks to every girl and who only wants to get into your pants. There will be time to date as you get older, so in the meantime - let's stay focused on your education and dreams. Boys can become a distraction and eventually you'll forget where you're going if you don't remain focused. It's time to continue our ride, look in the mirror and say; I Am Worth It!

Let's continue down *I Am Worth It Block* and when we get to *Smile* block, let's stop. We know there are times when you just don't feel like smiling. You may not want to smile because you may have had an argument with your family, peers, teachers or are just having a bad day. Don't let this keep you from smiling. When you smile, you brighten someone else's day. Now look in the mirror, turn that frown into a smile and say "I will keep a Smile on my beautiful face!"

We are half way there; before you pull off, make sure you fix your mirrors. Head towards *I Will Be Somebody Block* and when you arrive, let's just pull over and have a little talk. Life may not always go the way you want, no matter how much you try and try to stop things from happening. No matter what life throws at you, you must keep striving and move on. There is a future ahead of you and you will be somebody. You are already special to someone and that someone is you. You will be somebody in your community, home and school. Now look in the mirror with a smile and say I Will Be Somebody!

It's time to go and our ride is almost coming to an end. Time to fix the mirror again - but before you put the car in drive, how are your grades? I know! I know! You don't want to talk about school. School can be very challenging at times, especially as you enter higher grades. Well you may be the girl struggling in school, so never be afraid to ask for help - and remember there are no dumb questions. Everybody has different learning styles. It's not how you begin, but how you end. You are educated and smart - remember that.

You may be the girl who gets straight A's, makes honor roll every marking period and doesn't like being called a 'nerd'; just know that God created you to be different, He created you to excel in school. Now look in the mirror with a smile on your face and say I Am Educated and Smart!

Let's keep going - we are almost there, no time to stop now. Continue until you see *I Am A Leader* and *Not A Follower Block*. What makes you a leader? Are you a young girl who has influence over other girls? Do you inspire other girls? Lastly, are you setting an example for girls in your community, home and school?

Think about that for a minute as you drive. Now ask yourself, "Am I A Follower?" Leaders build followers who will eventually lead. Followers follow others and have no sense of direction. There may be times when you will need to follow someone - however make sure that person is a positive role model. I know you are a leader; repeat this with a smile on your face - I Am A Leader and Not A Follower!

I can't believe we've been driving for 7 blocks without music. Turn the radio on and let's play 'I'm Building My Confidence, by the 'Mirror Mirror Princess'. As you drive, do you see *I Am Not Who They Say I Am Block*? See that's the block where people try to tear you down. They say things like; 'you're dumb, stupid, ugly, skinny, fat, you're just like your mom and dad, nobody wants you around, you won't graduate, you'll have a baby and be a dropout or nobody will ever love you'. Well those are lies! Never believe the lies because you are not what they say. You are what God says you are. You are educated, smart and beautiful no matter your size; generational curses are broken over your life and you will not be a teenage mother. Remember God loves you! Keep smiling because you are almost there and remember, I Am Not Who They Say I Am!

As you approach a red light, I want you to slow down on *Never Give Up Block*. Building your confidence requires you to surround yourself with positive people and stay away from those who bring negativity. Smile every chance you get and give a compliment to others. Giving up is not an option; believe in yourself, get to know yourself and work on building your confidence daily because it doesn't come overnight. Look in the mirror with a smile and say I Will Never Give Up!

That was a long red light, but it was worth the wait. The light is now green so please proceed to You Are A Confident Princess block. You will see all the beautiful princesses outside awaiting your entrance. Go and celebrate with them, you made it! You are a Confident Princess!

Declare Everyday:

I AM BEAUTIFUL
I AM GOOD ENOUGH
I AM WORTH IT
I WILL KEEP A SMILE ON MY FACE
I WILL BE SOMEBODY
I AM EDUCATED & SMART
I AM A LEADER AND NOT A
FOLLOWER
AM NOT WHO THEY SAY I AM
I WILL NEVER GIVE UP
I AM CONFIDENT

About Lakisha Selby

Lakisha Selby was born and raised in Wilmington, Delaware. She is the mother of four beautiful and intelligent children. In May 2013, she received her Bachelor of Science Degree from Springfield College of Human Services in Wilmington, Delaware. She is currently enrolled at Wilmington University in Newcastle, Delaware pursuing her Master's Degree in Administration of Human Service. Lakisha is the founder of Women Of Courage, Inc. Women of Courage is a 501(c)(3) organization committed to empowering, inspiring, motivating and supporting young ladies and women from all walks of life through community outreach, education, mentoring, seminars, strategic alliance and workshops. Lakisha is dedicated to building confidence and self-esteem among young girls.

Lakisha's Acknowledgments

This chapter of the book is dedicated to my beautiful daughters, Diamond and Deionna Selby-Wing. I want them to know they are the most beautiful girls in the world and can be anything they set their mind to become. I dedicate this chapter to all the girls who struggle with their confidence and self-esteem. I love you all and I hope you enjoy this chapter of **The Princess in You**. Know that you are beautiful just the way you are. Walk into your community and school as if you own it, with your head held high.

Born to Lead; The Journey From a Princess to a Queen

by Marla Smith

"Do not think in your heart that you will escape in the king's palace any more than all the other Jews. For if you remain completely silent at this, relief and deliverance will arise for the Jews from another place, but you and your father's house will perish. Yet who knows whether you have come to the kingdom for such a time as this." **Esther 4:13-14 NKJV**

Do you know you were called for a great purpose? Are you aware that you were called for such a time as this; to be one who will change lives, a generation, a community or maybe even a nation? Do you know that you were born to lead? I'm sure you're probably thinking "Who...ME?!" YES, YOU!! God has called you to be great in this earth and you were purposed to stand out and stand up for God's glory. Often times, we think little of ourselves and even compare ourselves to others - never realizing the true potential and treasure lying inside waiting to be discovered and extracted. I began this journey by sharing how I discovered I was born to lead. I also shared the unique story of a young woman in the Bible who came from a modest, humble upbringing and later rose to a position of power that not only changed her life - but saved a nation. First, let me share a story you may or may not be familiar with - about a young woman named Queen Esther; a young woman who possessed strength, great courage and a desire to please God.

Esther - like yourself, was just an ordinary girl with an ordinary life, called for an extraordinary destiny. She was an orphaned Jewish girl also known as Hadassah (her Jewish name) meaning God chose and appointed her to deliver her people - the Israelites from their enemy. She experienced a drastic life change by becoming an orphan through the death of her parents. The Bible never mentions Esther having siblings, which indicates she may have been an only child. Could you imagine being alone, not having a mother or father in your life? Maybe some of you are experiencing this right now. Maybe your mother is absent from your life or even your father. Maybe you were put in situations you could not control, but wish you could change like Esther. It is during those times you may feel there isn't a purpose for your life, when God steps in to reveal His magnificent love for YOU and the greatness He has placed inside of you.

I'm sure as a young girl, Esther desired to change her situation; to have the continued love and attention of her parents. I'm sure she wanted to feel the embrace of her father and the gentle kiss and nurture of her mother each day. How could anyone possibly anticipate anything good coming from this situation? I imagine the feelings Esther experienced were nothing close to feeling like a princess or even seeing herself as a leader - but rather a lost child desiring the touch, love and support of her parents. The Bible says that when mother and father forsake you, the Lord will take care of you (Psalms 27:10, NKJV). Although Esther's life seemed bleak and unpromising, it is circumstances like this when God arrives and prepares a plan greater than one could ever imagine. In this moment of her life, God - by His loving hands, begins to mold her into the leader she will become. God sends someone who will not only mentor and teach her the ways of Christ - but will adopt and love her as their own daughter.

The person who came into Esther's life to raise and father her, was named Mordecai. He is her first cousin and nephew of her deceased father Abihail, who lived in a city called Babylon - ruled by a King named Ahasuerus (also known as King Xerxes). He took Esther in as his own child and unknowingly prepared her to become Queen.

Now, let me stop there with the story: it amazes me how God always makes sure His daughters are taken care of, even in circumstances which seem unfavorable and unfair - or when we can't see the treasure of who we are. Even with the devastating loss Esther experienced, God never left her alone. This reminds me of a time in my life as a teenager when I felt alone, worthless and lost. Though I was raised in church with both parents in my life, I experienced a lot of rejection and was plagued with depression. I always felt like I wasn't good enough and had very little confidence. I dealt with the secret war of not loving who God created me to be. Much of it was because I often compared myself to my friends, what TV and media said was beautiful or attractive and I rarely received affirmation and affection from my parents - though they were good parents. I often felt misunderstood and thought that if I looked differently or acted like someone other than myself - I would be valid, I would matter and would be relevant. I wanted to fit in, be noticed, be accepted - be loved.

I recall a time when I was in 5th grade and my class was outside for recess. Most of the time, I played with my friends, always smiling and appearing to be happy - but on this particular day, I couldn't keep the pain I had on the inside buried. I was overwhelmed with depressing emotions of rejection, low self-esteem and the pain of feeling alone and unworthy. I experienced hurtful words from others and pretended as if they didn't affect me, when in reality they wounded me. I remember sitting alone on an old wooden bench that was positioned between a big oak tree and baseball field fence. I sat there with feelings of despair, crying profusely. It was like I came to a place of questioning the point of my living. The day was a cool, lightly breezy. The sun was bright and the leaves turned colors; some had already fallen off the trees, proving that fall had arrived. I remember as I sat there, tears silently streaming down my face - head buried into my hands questioning God; "Why!?! Why me!?! Why do I have to suffer? Why did you bring me into this earth? What is my purpose!?!" It was all so real. I recall telling God I couldn't take it anymore, I just wanted to be happy. Why was I put on this earth?

Much like Esther, who experienced the pain of losing her parents and being alone; I was experiencing the pain of not knowing who I was and not living as the person God designed. During that time in my life, I could not see nor did I understand

God had a great purpose and call on my life. I was completely blinded by the lies and circumstances of my life and couldn't see the true essence and beauty of who I really was. That was the point where God began to change me and my life so I could truly see and know who I am. I was much like Esther; a hidden, undiscovered treasure destined to lead and become a Queen.

You may wonder how I went from feeling defeated and hopeless, to being a leader: well, just stay with me as I continue with Esther's journey. Though Esther experienced tragedy, she is raised by her cousin Mordecai who teaches her in the ways to honor God. Through Mordecai, God reveals to Esther who she is and the important role she will play in life. A decree is made; King Ahaseurus is in search of a new queen after Queen Vashti disobeyed his request. Esther enters a season of preparation; she's taken into the king's palace, where she is now under the care of Hegai who was responsible for looking after the virgin young women. What's most interesting is that Esther pleased Hegai and gains his favor. She gets the best room, the best choice of maidservants and even extra beauty preparations beyond what they were allowed to receive.

Certainly, she stood out among the other women because of the grace and favor God placed in her life. When God calls you to be a leader, often you will stand out and may feel like you don't fit in. However, you must understand that God has called you to not blend in or join the crowd -but to be different! It's wonderful to be different because you give people the opportunity of seeing the light of Christ in your life; you will become a beacon of hope for someone. You will serve as the role model many will look up to, because of the purpose on your life.

So, Esther's life-changing journey has begun. She conceals her identity as a Jew by the command of her adopted father and endures a year of preparation, which includes a purification process and several beauty preparations; afterwards, she is presented to the King. This was certainly a big deal, considering the young virgin women were only given one chance to impress the king. This was the opportunity of a lifetime! But God had a plan for Esther's life. It is important to note that before she presented herself before the king, she asked Hegai what would please the king and didn't request what the other young women requested. This shows the heart of a true leader. Esther wasn't concerned about looking like everyone else or being like them. She didn't have selfish motives, yet she exuded great confidence. Esther obtained the favor of the king and everyone saw she was chosen to be queen. Why? Because God chose her first and He created the beauty she possessed. The Bible described Esther as being lovely and beautiful (Psalms 4:7, NKJV).

I believe the beauty Esther possessed was not on the outside; it was a beauty she possessed inside. From the beginning of creation, everything God created was GOOD! You are His beautiful creation and masterpiece. You must remember that we are fearfully and wonderfully made. This is all a part of discovering who you are as a leader. I had to learn this for myself by seeing the value and worth of who I was. I realized I didn't appreciate the beauty I possessed. God began to pour His love on me and healed the broken places in my life. He showed me how to view myself from a new perspective. I chose to believe God had greater plans and that there was something great inside of me. This is what God wants you see about yourself. You're His daughter, His Princess!

Esther's greatest role and achievement wasn't just becoming a queen; there was purpose - a larger purpose beyond her benefit. A plot was devised to destroy her people by King Ahasaerus's general Haman. He influenced the king to believe they were the enemy and with the king's approval, set a plan in motion to destroy Esther's people. At this point in Queen Esther's life, this is when purpose meets destiny! She rises and becomes the leader she was born to be. Mordecai sends a message to Esther explaining that she was placed there 'for such a time as this'- to help save her people. Imagine the pressure Esther was under, facing the reality that the lives of her people was in jeopardy and she was the only one who could do save them?

Who could save her people from the threat of extinction, while facing the reality of possibly losing her own life? She risks her life twice to save her people by going before the king - her husband, without permission after hearing Haman's plan to assassinate the Jews. Keep in mind that what Esther did was a dangerous act. Anyone who approached the king without his permission was against the law and was punished by death. Despite the odds against her, Esther understood her purpose. This was the moment she discovered and understood the greatness she possessed. She knew she had the power to bring change. Though she was willing to risk her life, God's favor protected Queen Esther and deliverance was her nation!

You were called to be a leader for your generation for such a time as this! Many times we discount ourselves of the true abilities God has given us as His leaders and agents of change. You must dare to believe and trust God in what He says you are, for the Greater one lives on the inside of you and with Christ all things are possible. So now it's time to rise up Princess and be the leader you were born to be!

Born to Lead: The Leader in You Activity

"Remember that God has specifically placed you here for a purpose and He has called you to be a leader, a Princess, that He has uniquely created and designed you to be. He loves you and nothing can separate YOU from the love of Jesus Christ".
(Romans 8:39)

Take a moment write down words of Who You Are as a born leader. Have fun!

SPEAK LIFE OVER YOURSELF EVERYDAY!

Write Words of Affirmation of Who You Are as God's Chosen Leader:

I Am...

_____

_____

_____

_____

_____

_____

_____

_____

_____

I Will...

_____
_____
_____
_____
_____
_____
_____

I Know...

_____
_____
_____
_____
_____
_____
_____

I Have...

_____
_____
_____
_____
_____
_____
_____

Born to Lead Princess Prayer

Father, I believe you created me and have called me for a
unique purpose. As you did with Esther, I pray that you
will bless me indeed and reveal your plan and purpose for
my life so that I may walk with the grace, confidence,
beauty and the power you have placed inside of me so
that I may know who I am in YOU! Prepare me to be the
leader you called me to be in Jesus' Name, Amen!

BORN TO LEAD PRINCESS DAIRY:

WHAT I BELIEVE...

_____

_____

_____

_____

_____

_____

_____

_____

_____

Royally Signed By:

_____

Date: _____

About Marla

Marla is a Youth Pastor of Prophetic Kingdom Ministries where she works and ministers to youth. She also ministers through song and is a part of the praise and worship team. She recently joined a new movement in to support the self-esteem of young girls and young women by being a featured speaker for the 1st and 2nd Annual Queen in You Conference. As a single woman, Marla is very passionate about mentoring young ladies and grooming them to identify who they are and their purpose. Outside of ministry, Marla works for a non-profit organization working with students within Milford, De where she resides. She has four siblings.

Marla's Acknowledgements

I would like to first give honor and praise to my Lord and Savior of my life, Jesus Christ, who has blessed me with this great opportunity. If it wasn't for His unconditional love, grace and His unmerited favor, I would not be here and who I am today - a Queen!! I am so grateful to God for the wonderful things He has done in my life! I'm looking forward to the great things God has in store. This is the beginning of the greater! I would also like to thank and honor my mother and father; I love you both. Thank you for teaching me the way of Christ and His character. I would like to thank my sister, Andrea Griffin for your undying love and support. Apostle Jermaine Johnson and Pastor Roberta Johnson. Thank you for believing in me. You both are a true treasure in my life.

To all my family, my PKM church family and all of my friends; you know who you are - can't name you all, but I LOVE you all so much! Last, but not least - I would like to give a special thanks to Dr. Kishma George for allowing me to be a part of this amazing project! May God bless you Woman of God. Thank You for seeing the gift of God in me, I am honored by this opportunity!

Rules of Royalty

by Danielle L. Ashley

Once upon a time in a society similar to today's, there were many versions of Beyoncé, Nicky Minaj and the Kardashians - but there is only one Princess. She is marked; a true beauty. It sets her apart from the rest. When she enters a room, elegance radiates from her very being and she automatically stands out in a crowd. She owns the room with her grace and her quiet confidence. Magically, she sparkles where ever she goes because royalty flows through her veins. Her spirit shines like the sun on a warm spring day because it's pure, lovely and admirable. Not only does her spirit shine - so does her crown. Each ruby, each diamond; every color brightens and illuminates every time she turns her head. She is careful to never let her chin down and always keeps her head up because she knows her crown could slip and fall to the ground.

She is unbothered by negativity and the opinions of others. She is a binding force of generosity and unselfishness - never biting, bitter or cutting. She surrounds herself with nothing but greatness. She is very careful of the company she keeps, for she knows they are representation of her character. She soars only with eagles. A princess is a purpose-driven individual with a warrior mentality. She carries herself in such a way that even if her world were falling apart into pieces, she would pick up each piece and rebuild. She stares adversity in the face and conquers it with kindness.

The princess recognizes the beauty of being in the moment; being unrushed and the beauty of sitting still. She also knows when to move in the shadows; the shadows aren't dark and gloomy, they are a covering for her introduction. It sets the moment for her extraordinary debut. Her exterior is an extension of her inward dignity. It's her total makeup; the makeup of her destiny. She looks graceful and beautiful from every angle. She is dignified; the crème de la crème of refinement. She is developed, polished and full of grace.

"If you are a princess, you should look like a princess" is the motto she lives by. This isn't something she switches on and off. This is her lifestyle which she lives, talks and breathes. There are Rules of Royalty to the life and style of a Princess. The first thing you should know is **The Princess doesn't try to be the center of attention.** Instead her grace, elegance, her style and confidence command the attention of every person in the room. Not only does the princess command attention when she enters the room - she also commands her morning. Before her feet hit the ground she cloths herself with a prayer and Scripture. After she declares her day, she visualizes how she wants to see herself for the day. Colors, textures and prints are just a few of her options. She wants to select the best choice because she knows she is putting forth her personal best presentation to the world. The wardrobe of a princess is powerful, professional and elegant. A princess is always in the spotlight, so she should routinely look well put together and classy even when dressing casually. It is very important to know the rule that **All Assets Should be kept Covered.** You should leave little to the imagination.

So say 'no' to the mini-skirt and super low-cut neckline. Say 'yes' to lace, wrap dresses, blazers, coat dresses, a-lined skirts, trench coats, classic patent leather pumps, ballet flats, neutrals and pastels. These styles cultivate an air of elegance. In a princesses' wardrobe - there are some 'must haves'; there are the pieces a princess must not live without. A 'must have' in a princess wardrobe would be a tailored suit. Dress suits are an important part of your collection. They embody confidence, power and professionalism. How awesome is it for a princess to walk into a room with one on? She means business when she wears one.

Here are some additional **Royalty Wardrobe Essentials** which are very beneficial to your Princess collection:

1. A White button up shirt
2. A Black Blazer
3. Dark Denim Jeans
4. LBD (Little Black Dress)
5. Black Jeans
6. Black Pumps
7. Ballet Flats

All of these pieces are timeless items that can be worn together or separately to create a regal, chic look for a royal princess. These pieces can be mixed and matched with other items you already have in your wardrobe. As a helpful nugget when you are getting dressed daily and going shopping think; Kate Middleton, Grace Kelly and Princess Diane (google them if you don't know who they are). They are all great inspirations regarding how to carry yourself as a princess. Remember - understated, elegance and simplicity are all key. A princess should always keep her appearance classy. Use makeup that looks natural. Keep your hair maintained and your nails manicured and simple.

So, we have covered the princesses' appearance and wardrobe - but what would the life and style of a princess be like without accessories? We can't forget accessories. Without some sparkle, shine and some bling-bling - life and style would be pretty dull. It would be no fun at all! A princess has to accompany her beautiful crown with earrings to die for, a necklace which is memorizing and bedazzled bracelets. Accessories are the final touches to complete your look – similar to the icing on a cake. But be very careful Princess, accessories are a 'make or break' item. It is very important to accessorize each outfit the correct way. Never pile on the jewels. If you are wearing a simple top or dress - then add a statement necklace, earrings or cocktail ring. Just be sure to not over accessorize. Remember - less is more in some cases.

The Most Important Rules of Royalty Are:

1. **Always remain true to yourself**: Be the best authentic version of yourself. No one is better at being you than you and that is your superpower.

2. **Individualize yourself**: Create a style that is your signature. Fashion says 'me too'; style says 'only me'. There are no carbon copy princesses allowed! Your style is a way to say who you are, without having to speak. Concentrate on creating your own individual style - a look that works best for you. Study and know what your strengths and weaknesses are. Always accentuate your strengths (best features). Know your size, wear it well and confidently.

3. **Always Set the Bar High**: Never dim your light and never worry about overdressing. A Princess is never uniformed with everyone else. Go out of the door boldly. Remember - first impressions are lasting impressions.

4. **Be Memorable**: Set a trend. Make others want to dress like you and be like you. People should always feel empowered and inspired when leaving your company.

You are now aware there are Rules of Royalty for being a princess. You know how a Princess should carry herself, how she should dress, how she acts - but the most important thing you should know and never forget, is that you are Beautiful inside out no matter what. No matter your shape, no matter your size, no matter your skin tone and no matter anyone's opinion. You are marvelously made. You are breathtaking, body and soul!

Dear Princess, no one can take your crown. It has been bought and paid for - so wear it well and with confidence. Being a princess is a lifestyle; this is what you were born to do. You are second to none, a style icon and an inspiration to all. Settling is not in your dictionary. Only the absolute best for the Princess. The time has come for all Princesses to make their mark on the world with their style and grace. So adjust your crown and fluff your hair. Shoulders back, chest high, feet apart, head up and Strut! Rise Up and Shine Princess - the world is your runway and it's waiting for you.

The Princess Style Daily Checklist

1. Am I wearing Confidence?
2. Do I have a smile on my face?
3. Is My Chin Up?
4. Are My Shoulders back and my Chest Up?
5. Did I wear my invisible crown?
6. Is my hair combed and in place?
7. Are my assets covered? Am I leaving little to the imagination?
8. Are my clothes wrinkle free?
9. Is my nail polish chipped?
10. Am I rocking my own personal style?
11. Am I looking my very best and giving my best presentation to the world?

*Be sure to check this list every day before leaving the house Princess!

About Danielle L. Ashley

A native of Dover, Delaware; Danielle is a lover of God, family and fashion. She is a loving mother of one son - Israel Marion, who keeps her busy and on her toes. Danielle is the daughter of Apostle James and Pippa Ashley. She is the leader of the Liturgical Dance Ministry (Revealing Divine Glory) and sings on the Praise and Worship Team at the Greater Life Christian Church. She also serves as an adjutant to Lady Pippa Ashley. In her spare time, she enjoys spending time with her son and family, traveling, singing, shopping and styling individuals to look their best. Danielle graduated from Dover High School in 2002. She attended Delaware State University and Harris School of

Business where she received her Medical Assistant Certification. She currently mentors for K.I.S.H. Home, Inc. and is a personal stylist.

Danielle's Acknowledgements

To my Savior, my Lord and Jesus Christ, thank You for this opportunity. Thank You for choosing me to be a voice heard by so many young beautiful girls. To my parents, Apostle James Ashley Jr. and Pastor Pippa Ashley. Thank you for your guidance, correction and love. To one of the most handsome, most stylish and most athletic young men I know; Israel J. Marion. I am so blessed to be your mom. I love you. To my brothers, James and Jarrius. Thank you for always protecting and loving your only sister. To my niece and nephew, your auntie loves you. To the entire Ashley and Guy family; I love you all. To the Marion and Johnson family; thank you for all of your love and support over the years -I love you all.

To my grandmother - the Queen Ruth Guy, I love you. To the Greater Life Christian Church family; I love you all, let's build the city. To my second set of parents; Bishop Joann and Willie White and the entire Rehoboth Family, I love you all. To my best friend and sister, Melissa Green. I absolutely love and cherish you. Thank you for your continuous support, your prayers and your love. Miles mean nothing to us. To my sister, Tiffany Smith; what would we do without each other? You are an inspiration! Thank you for your prayers, continuous support and love. To my sister Shanika Bell; you are an amazing woman, sister and friend. You are definitely one of my rocks. Thank you for never judging me, letting me be me and for always supporting, praying for me and loving me. You are truly a big sister, I have never had. To Dr. Kishma George; the visionary, entrepreneur, powerhouse and mogul in the making. Thank you for believing in me. Thank you for your prayers, your love and your push. You are truly an inspiration! To every princess in the world; you are beautiful, you are amazing and you are loved. Chin and Crowns Up!

The Dynasty Mind

by Tammy Collins Markee

Ring, Ring, Tambourine! If only I had a tambourine in my hand, the sound would lead me into a song and dance which would forever remain in my heart and make a difference in this world. Do you hear the sound of the tambourine? Dynasty calls out to you. The sleeping flame has risen.

The Dynasty Mind has awakened to dance toward the light and the sound of the music is igniting you by calling the sweet sound of your name, bringing a new song to your heart. The School of the Dynasty of Dreamers is ready to build your character; the prerequisite courses are designed to teach you - the student, all you need to know regarding the journey of success. Your name is associated with the ring of honor. You are a young woman of empowerment, like Miriam the Prophetess in the history of God's Word.

"*Then Miriam the prophetess, the sister of Aaron, took a tambourine in her hand, and all the women went out after her with tambourines and dancing. And Miriam sang to them: 'Sing to the Lord, for He has triumphed gloriously; the horse and his rider He has thrown into the sea.*" (Exodus 15:20-21) (ESV)

Become a confident woman with the courage to wait on God, leading a Dynasty of Women to celebrate each other's success. Step onto the Royal Highway which leads to stellar innovations.

The inner you has an entrepreneurial spirit. Fashion yourself into excellence by removing all distractions and become the epitome of those igniting moments which usher in an extraordinary investment towards your future. You possess the divine tapestry to weave a cloak of destiny for your own shoulders; the new, inner you is a necessary and key element for your walk in faith as an entrepreneur.

Start to dig deeper to accelerate the productivity lying within you. Enter gloriously into your own ring of inspiration. If you had a drum, would you beat it to a different rhythm? Champion others to live in their own freedom. Help your sisters to bring out the creativity of their minds and launch them firmly on the path to economic prosperity.

Start to become the Princess Archetype for a Dynasty of Entrepreneurs - which has a strong voice in our nation, helping to create jobs to eliminate poverty. Become a confident woman who trusts God like Miriam in the Bible and believe that God can perform a miracle in your life. Above all, start to prepare for your journey to the Promised Land.

You are engineered and built to offer great ideas and guide your peers. Your mandate is to inspire the youth of this generation to have an enterprising mind. Your divine assignment is to display uncommon goodwill to mankind. Did you know that a giver can never be barren? Become a fully-functioning individual who will come into her own timeless, never-ending and eternally-engaging flow of success.

Commence action to improve and sharpen your mind. You are the handiwork of God, built to attain the peak of perfection. The Princess in YOU was designed to dedicate her love walk to a fine degree of exploration and illumination - such that you will be greeted at the Pavilion of the ultra-luxe dynasty of high achievers.

Extraordinary dynasty ladies have high anticipation - therefore, much will be expected of you. So, you will need to master how to dispel the fears of underperforming, cobb-web mentalities -both in yourself and in others.

Brace for the birth of your dreams and prepare your spirit for the journey of the relentless pursuit of your success. Life's many blessings will surely establish you in an intricate laser-cut design of the adventure. On your fantastic voyage to the four-corner regions of the world, you will develop new tokens of friendships, a state of bliss and the momentum you will need to navigate your way towards the right dynasty of dreamers at the birthing port of your ship.

Expressed very simply, you deserve the best. Contrary to popular belief - your life's pursuit is to spring into action in order to enhance other peoples' lives by challenging those seasons of human existence which are filled with the pains of life. In due season, you will gain the courage to wait on God. Life's valuable lessons will teach you how to be wise. Always walk in faith and expectation. Know yourself and learn to align yourself in God's direction. Ask God to bless your creativity with witty inventions and ideas that are specially manufactured for a Dynasty of Creation.

"*I am Lady Wisdom, and I live next to Sanity; Knowledge and Discretion live just down the street*". (Proverbs 8:12-24) (MSG)

The Fear of God means hating Evil - whose ways I hate with a passion; pride, arrogance and crooked talk. Good counsel and common sense are my characteristics; I am both Insight and the Virtue to live by. With my help - leaders rule and lawmakers legislate fairly. With my help - governors govern with legitimate authority.

I love those who love me; those who look for me find me. Wealth and Glory accompany me, along with substantial Honor and a Good Name. My benefits are worth more than a big salary; my returns exceed any imaginable bonus. You can find me on Righteous Road; that's where I walk - at the intersection of Justice Avenue. I hand out life to those who love me, filling their arms with armloads of life!

Life is full of trials and triumph, but know that you are not alone in your quest along your desired career path. You have to eliminate self-sabotage patterns. Remember that every stressful situation has an expiration date.

Develop a spirit of giving. Understand the financial strategies for eliminating debt and obtain money through God's way. King David - the man after God's own heart, gave $1,000 and his giving stopped the plague for an entire nation.

"And they sacrificed sacrifices unto the Lord, and offered burnt offerings unto the Lord, on the morrow after that day, even a thousand bullocks, a thousand rams, and a thousand lambs, with their drink offerings, and sacrifices in abundance for all Israel." 1 Chronicles 29:2 (KJV)

Your trees are producing good fruit. No matter what you are pursuing, keep a humble and humane spirit. Expand your knowledge and understand other cultures. Develop efficient self-awareness for articulating your thought processes with dignity, esteem and enthusiasm. Explore every facet of knowledge and obtain a firm grasp of relevant facts, figures and words that will afford you the opportunity for advancement on all fronts. In entrepreneurship, become the Founder and Proprietress of your own Dynasty.

The undeniable fact is that you must always carefully study the Terms, Conditions and Disclosures of any contract. Strive to live in economic independence by choosing to invest wisely. Come into self-discovery, which allows you to attain an attitude of gratitude for your own soul and the souls of others. Approach life and living with a fundamental attitude of integrity, respect, civility, character, clarity, composure, appropriateness and politeness. Develop upfront, a mindset of world class performance. Insist on looking ahead to a bright future. Know that you are a breathing, living flame of hope and inspiration. In your total devotion to God, He has prepared His Princess for Greatness.

Ultimately, you are establishing and stating your intent to become a true source of inspiration for sisterhood all over the world. Connect with the throbbing pulse of the nation. Become a lady who is well-prepared, self-sufficient and self-propelled to keep her eye on the mark of accomplishment. The dollar dynamics of economic growth and development are things you must learn. Refuse to get caught up in the world's trends to avoid being misled or distracted. Choose to continually empower others through your giving. The Princess in YOU should dig her heels firmly into the ground and with the Holy Royal Crown firmly planted on your head, prepare to give strength to others.

The Princess in YOU sends out thoughts of love, peace and prosperity to mankind. With her pristine record, she renders the truth to peel back layers of her unselfish acts. She is a pioneer of reform, striving hard not only to make a healthy income - but to possess the financial strength and responsibility for leading others to their own wealth.

A Lady of Wisdom; she takes a page from her book of knowledge and teaches the world to scale towards heights of rich spiritual and material, personal freedom. Being an excellent money manager; she takes time to extinguish the flames of economic chaos, thereby creating a force for recycling financial growth into the lives of others. Her ability to make rational financial decisions will inevitably start a movement for other ladies; it will not diminish the worth of the Princess in themselves, however. Her journey to the place where she speaks as a woman full of wisdom and as an emerging leader with a voice which turns frustration into hope, has begun.

The Princess in You serves as a willing vessel of honor. She will study the historical greats who had Dynastic Empires. The Queen of Sheba's Royal visit to the wise man called King Solomon is eloquent testimony to the fact that any woman who aspires greatness must seek it at the feet of the wise. She was already a thriving force in the trade of gold, fragrances and rare gems. King Solomon himself, had an astronomical magnitude of wisdom and combined this with a deep and uncommon knowledge of God. He was also skilled in commerce and trade and built a fleet of ships. He crafted shields of hammered gold which were stored in the House of Forest of Lebanon.

The Princess in YOU comes from the lineage of a Dynasty of Dreamers. The Dynasty Mind possesses outstanding interpersonal skills that are not only endearing to others; they can arouse gifts, talents and ultimately a sense of destiny within them. The opportunities that are possible through the Lady of Wisdom allow her to stay on the Righteous Road towards engaging her passion of life and helping others live by design - not by spurious chance.

She advances steadily on Justice Avenue, while doing all things to the glory of God's Kingdom. Her passion never ceases and she continues as a performance-driver by developing success potential in her people.

Dynasty Lady, you owe it to future generations to establish a good track record of encouraging well-structured, thriving and successful businesses. You can successfully market your services - even among unfair competition, as a small business owner. You can commit to a long-term career resulting in wealth for attaining anything in your life. The opportunity is waiting for you to possess a steady cash flow for financial opportunities. Refuse to be scared of taking risks. Cultivate an enthusiastic attitude and effervescent personality which are the key elements to a winning Dynasty. The world needs to know you are a world-changer, a firepower dreamer and the architect of your own destiny.

Embedded in the soil of your soul is a fertile mind; you must cultivate the soil, in order to steer your way towards roaring success. In essence, this artistry will aid you to flourish in the harvesting of the Master's Sacred Wisdom. Your journey to enlightenment will honor your earning potential. Therefore, start reconditioning your mind to establish the set of constructive choices leading to your beautiful economic destiny.

Become a Master Strategist who inspires your imagination and steers your life for positive self-growth. Take that leap of faith which allows you to utilize the Principles of Budgeting. Embark on a mission that furnishes you with the keen strategy of obtaining multiple streams of income and revenue so that in unsettling economic times, you are prepared to weather the storm of uncertain market returns.

You are a born legacy-builder of adventures and a female figure who will heighten the awareness of nations of Princesses who have developed the capacity to empower others. In that quest, you will show reverence and respect for every man, woman and child.

Impart a sense of teamwork building and the noble characteristic of human creativity to dynasty newcomers.

The Pilgrimage to Self-Love Discovery Starts with you; The Princess in YOU as the Leader!

20 Small Business Ideas for Young Enterprising Minds:
1. Become a Virtual Assistant
2. Non-Profit Work
3. Forex Trading
4. Buying and Selling on EBay
5. Bakery Business
6. Start a Teen Magazine
7. Teen Radio Talk Show
8. Computer Repair
9. Greeting Card Creations
10. Photography
11. App Development
13. Gift Baskets
14. Jewelry Design
15. Investment
16. Garage Sales
17. Art Collections
18. Blogging
19. YouTube Pod Cast
20. Baby-Sitting Services

Instructive: Strategic Plan of Action for the Execution of Business Goals
"Failing to Plan is a Plan to Fail"- Alan Lakein

Questions to Consider:

1. What type of business do you plan to execute?

2. What are your plans for the future financial growth of the business?

3. How well are you mentally preparing to become a Good Steward over your financial profits?

Write and Implement a Comprehensive Plan:

- o Written Visions, Goals and Objectives
- o Maintain your financial Heath
- o Direction of Future Growth
- o Elevate the Quality of your Life
- o Source of Funding
- o Project List
- o Leadership Action Plan for Productive Connections
- o Seek Wise Counsel
- o Learn and Exhibit Good Communication Skills
- o Target Audience/Marketing Networking Matrix
- o Assessment Angles
- o Where are you are now?
- o What will trending business developments look like in months, and 8 years to come?
- o What is the next step in your business?
- o What are the perspective of others who do not know your business strategy?
- o Good Stewardship
- o Life of Discipleship
- o Study the Wisdom of King Solomon in the book of Proverbs and Ecclesiastes

Create an atmosphere of mutual respect. Promote a climate of peace and live a life of ease. Never allow anyone to sabotage your future. Insist on engaging your Dynasty Mind through a higher level of consciousness. Become an expert in the art of creative visualization. As you mature, life's lessons will help you become willing and ready to be a young woman with a servant's heart.

If you traced the heritage of Royal Women, you will discover nothing but rich legacies of wisdom, beauty and creativity. These women were unstoppable. Queen Esther's wisdom and courage in risking her life to save a nation is a perfect example of the nobility of these great women. She was a God-Fearing woman living in a pagan court.

The man in her life does not define a Women of God. She is defined by God in her life, as exemplified by the loyalty of the woman Ruth, ancestress of Christ. Ruth was confident in the blessings of God after her husband died and even until the man of destiny found her - her Boaz. Her obedience brought her rich rewards.

As your Dynasty Mind ascends towards the Heavens, always let the light from your lamp illuminate your mind and all those around you. Never allow anyone to remove the Oil from your Lamp!

Blaze Forth Dynasty Mind! Blaze Forth!

About Tammy Collins Markee

Right Honorable Tammy Collins Markee is a native of New Orleans, but currently resides in Houston, Texas. In humble submission to a life of divine mandate, Tammy is lovingly dedicated to her primary calling as an Evangelist/Prophet. She holds a Degree from Dillard University, with a major in Urban Planning/Public Policy and concentration in Political Science and Social Work. Tammy was nominated for the United States Presidential Award for Literacy; featured in the Louisiana Weekly Newspaper for winning the JC Penney's Community Service Award for Literacy and appointed by Mayor Marc H. Morial to serve on the New Orleans Criminal Justice Council.

She is an International Human Rights Activist, Entrepreneur and Writer. A brief sojourn in Europe, where she valiantly advocated against racial discrimination and police brutality, led to her appointment as International Affairs Director by Pastor Kenneth Glasgow - brother of Rev. Al Sharpton, a celebrated American Activist. Pastor Kenneth Glasgow is Founder of T.O.P.S.; The Ordinary People Society. Tammy was appointed to the Board of Governors of The Global Institute for Human Excellence by Prince (Dr.) Yomi Garnett, the Institute's President. Also, she is appointed Ambassador to We Care for Humanity by Princess Maria Amor. Tammy is the Business Manager/Literary Agent to Prince (Dr.) Yomi Garnett, Celebrated Host of the Voice America Talk Show, "Dream The Life; Live The Dream." VOICE AMERICA has over 4.5 Million listeners, with High Profile Guest Speakers from all over the world. Tammy is a Columnist for K.I.S.H. Magazine (Dynasty of Dreamers) & (Celebration of Excellence) with Dr. Yomi Garnett.

Tammy is protégé of Leonard Stanley Chaikind, Founder of Institutional Investors Consulting Company, IICC and a Goodwill Ambassador for the Small Business Today Magazine. Tammy has been appointed by Madame Sabine Balve - Founder/President of the World Leaders Forum Dubai (WLFD) as Business Development Manager/Media Relations. She is the Executive Producer for Bunny DeBarge and Skee Skinner (Film Producer) and Business Manager for Johnathan Haggerty (NFL), King Wawa (Haitian Musician) and Gisele Haralson (Film Producer/Author).

ENDORSEMENTS

"*Tammy Collins Markee hit the nail right on the head with this brilliant and insightful chapter. The only route to authentic success is to arrive at the realization that you are the ultimate author of your own destiny. You are the captain of the ship of your own destiny. No one can steer this ship on your behalf. Therefore, she is calling out to you to grab your steering wheel and navigate your ship of success into the uncharted waters of a glorious Dynasty, where you, and only you, are the Princess of your own Kingdom!*"

HRH Yomi Garnett, MD
CEO
Royal Biographical Institute, Philadelphia, Pennsylvania.

Tammy's Acknowledgements:

First and Foremost, I humbly thank God for the honor and privilege to share this chapter, The Dynasty Mind, with the world. I am also grateful for the rare privilege of sharing the same literary platform with Dr. Kishma A. George, My Beloved Sister-in-Christ, I appreciate your priceless inspiration and support in giving me the platform to express my Vision of Global Fraternity. *The Princess in YOU* is clearly evident to all who work shoulder to shoulder with you to spread Love, Light and Loyalty to our God and Father throughout the world.

Also, my Special Thanks go to; Dr. Tracy Quintana, ChosenButterfly Publishing and the gifted Co-Authors of the book **The Princess in YOU**. A book only earns its status as a literary work of value at the esteemed pleasure of its readership. Therefore, I sincerely express a word of gratitude to the readers of **The Princess in YOU.**

This chapter is dedicated to my loving and supportive Mother, Father, Grandparents and Family, who have been the fountain of my legacy. Thank you for helping me to soar with the eagles. I love you all! I also dedicate this to the Loving Memory of my beloved sister, the late Dr. Twanna Collins, the Princess who will forever live in my heart. I will always be a Dynasty Dreamer because of YOU!

Finally, I would like to thank the Legendary Hank Moore for acknowledging me in his book,

Pop Icons and Business Legends.
God Bless You All!

Special Thanks to: Elmonia F. Collins, Dr. John Alderson, DC,CCN, Sonya Gross, Eugene Mikle, Elder Thomas & Barbara Cole, HRH Yomi Garnett M.D. (Voice America Radio Network), Julie Jones, M.D., Princess Moradeun Ogunlana, Co-Authors of the book, *Dreaming the Dream,* Dr. Dorothy Butler, Reverend Hon. Lillie Y. Dunbar & Family, Dr. Chyna Bethley, Felicia McKnight, Tymoo Brown, Jakeia Porter, Randie Williams, Kari Wilson, Marcella Rodriguez Guidroz, Theresa Peters-Fisher, Gloria Williams Burras, Clareesa Shields (Gold Medalist), Retha Bryant, Angela Zeigler, Dr. Jacqueline Weatherly, Prophet Laron Matthews, Dr. Connye Bryant, Rosa Dean Grau, Queen Williams, Tressie Pete, Kenneth & Mae Pete, Earl & Terrinita

Smith & Family, Lottie Stamper, Cynthia Y. Sandifer, LTanya Clarks Johnson, Becca Pierce, Trinese Jordan Duplessis, Demeatria D. Haggerty, and Dr. Doniel Ervin.

Dr. Nicoline Ambe, Milton & Elder Doris Langston, Pastor Henry Bolden, Hon. Marie Williams, Donna Britt, Demetrice Kennedy, Lucy Hunter, H.E. Ambassador Kelly Fawaz, Raymond Ricner, Nellie Y. Jones, Gisele Haralson, Kelly Price, Devika Parikh, Diane Butler, Chante Moore, Loureva W. Slade, Trisha Mann-Grant, Evette Holyfield, Nolbert Brown, Jr., Tasha Jackson, Janina Silas, Lashawna Million, Durell Jacque, Elder Broderick Holbert, H.E. Tony Taylor, Sandman AKA (Sandmeezy), Anthony Broussard, Mack Spears, Josephine M. Shelby, Stephanie Yvette Norman, Sherie Lewis, Dionne Dameron, Tammy Kling, Drs. Lewis & Shamira Brown, Connie Alexander, Chris Elliot, Raymond Steiner, Noralyn Banda, Lisa Collins, Meagan Gross and Tara Michelle Artis

Parinaz; a Boutique- (Rohit and Ashuman Garg), Texa Cali Studios-(Photographers: Ro Ferrier and Raul R. Leal), and Jocelyn Island-(MakeupArtist).

Mallami A. Kayode, Dozie C. Ugochukwu, Tamika D. Nelson, Mica Scott, Kim Landers, Amanda Lee Jackson Alkananey, Teresa Michelle Ulmer, La'reka Marshall (Publicist), Tammy Lynn Glapion, Twana McClure Smith, Tokiwa Scott, Zelda Dashiell, Marquita Y. Clay, Trina Y. Price, Linda Collins-Cage, Frances Turner, Linda F. Tate, Jackie Cherry, Patricia Jackson, Deviney Jackson, Desiree Riggins, Josephine M. Shelby, Latoya Veal, Wendy Nacol, Kandace Lewis, Ilka Ricks, Rajput Gkumar, Steve

Patt, Frances Turner, Linda F. Tate, Dr. Charles Clark, Naila Husain Chowdhury, Nathifa Olufemi (Fiona Moore Shanks), Dinah Sam, Yolanda Marks, Vanessa Hopkins, Homer Cornish, Paul Geary, Tammy George, Tammy Lee White, Adrienne Dickerson Jopes, Rosemary Buckner, Demetra Nelson, Dionne C. Haydel, Dionne Thipado Parharm, James Gosa, Michelle Jarrell-James, Felicia Jarrell, Jay Ray, Raneisha Brignac, Tracey Harris, Benjamin Musunza, Deanna Chapman Granger, Nicole Chapman Granger, Angelia Brown, Terrel Garvie, Major Miguel Reece, Dr. Shon Neyland, Rick Reese, Cordine Williams, Arcelia Armstrong, Alina Sztankovits, Leanne Marston, Theresa Bullock Smith, Beatrice Damond, Thelma Padron, Ellaina Shedrick, Kristen Byas, Eliza C. Parham, Vickey Parham, Crown Collins, Raikeya J. Collins, Albert Collins, and Prinstena, Poetry & (Princeton) Collins

Dream Big!

by Kishma A. George

This chapter covers the last aspect of the PRINCESS in YOU! The princess in YOU is not simply beautiful, graceful, elegant but is also a DREAMER! As a dreamer, you should dream BIG! DREAM BIG! Yes, dreaming BIG is also the princess in YOU! You should strive to reach the stars. The PRINCESS in YOU should not hold you back from achieving YOUR DREAMS, BIG dreams but rather propel you to explore life to make a difference in the world. To make a difference in the lives of people. You should have a GREAT desire to leave a mark, yes, your MARK in the world.

"Write the vision, and make it plain upon tables, that he may run that readth it. For the vision is yet for an appointed time, but at the end it shall speak, and not lie; though it tarry wait for it; because it will surely come, it will not tarry,"(Habakkuk 2: 2-3, KJV).

Many times, we lose sight of our God-given purpose! Most of us have dreams and goals we aspire to achieve, but often we inadvertently allow life's circumstances to move these visions aside. God showed Abram a vision that he would have as many children as stars in the sky. At that time, Abram was old and without children, but Abram believed God! He had faith in God's promise. To have faith in God is to trust Him. Hebrews 11:1 says; "Now faith is the substance of things hoped for the evidence of things not seen."

Has God ever showed you a vision? What was your response to the vision? Did you believe what God showed you in the vision? One day during my prayer time, He showed me a vision where He wanted me to produce an inspirational stage play to empower people to pursue their God-given dreams. I laughed. God, are You serious? I told God I had not taken acting, nor drama classes in college and that I have never written a stage play in my life. When I left the prayer room, I called my mom and told her what God wanted me to do. Her response was, "Yes, you can do all things through Christ who strengthens you." My baby leaped inside of me.

Remember to share your dreams with only those who will EMPOWER, MOTIVATE and INSPIRE you to birth your God-given dreams. The following month, I kept my ears to the pulse of God for direction regarding how to put the stage play production together. As I moved by faith, the doors began to open. I partnered with two other great women who had a wonderful story and the stage play was created: When You Have a DREAM. I was super excited! God sent the cast members, the location and the stage play songs. Thus, the script fell in place.

I want to encourage you that when you have a dream, do not give up! When your dream seems impossible and you are struggling to overcome challenges standing in your way, remember that your God moves mountains! When you have a

Dream, YOU have to disconnect from people who disrespect your God-given dreams and drain your energy. Surround yourself with people who believe in you, inspire you and motivate you towards reaching your vision, dreams, goals and destiny! You have to guard your mind against dream-killers and distance yourself from the small-minded and negative people who want to pull you down. Having positive relationships and the right people in your life will empower you to reach your highest potential in God.

When you have a dream, to take leaps of FAITH! God wants you to step out on faith and believe you can write that book, open up a business, a clothing line, sing, write a play or become the class president: don't wait! With God, nothing is impossible! JUST BELIEVE and TRUST GOD! There are no limitations with God! He has no limits! Whatever VISION He showed you, stand on His Word; PRAY and FAST for guidance - Do not give up no matter what it looks like in the physical realm. God can do exceeding abundantly above all we can ask or think!

Keep PUSHING! Keep DREAMING! Don't give up! It's time to change the world with your DREAM! God has called you to DREAM so He may use you to CHANGE the WORLD and make a difference in the lives of others! Remember, DREAM BIG! It's YOUR TIME!

In conclusion, it is hoped that YOU have found the DREAMER in the PRINCESS in YOU! That you are ready to let yourself DREAM BIG! STAND tall and be confident and ready to handle your BIG DREAMS like the PRINCESS that YOU are!

Yes, the PRINCESS in YOU is ready like never before to conquer the WORLD!!

The Princess in You Dreams Journal!

Write down all the dreams you would like to achieve this year.

_____
_____
_____
_____
_____
_____
_____
_____
_____

What is the mission for your dream?

_____
_____
_____
_____
_____
_____
_____
_____
_____
_____
_____

What is the vision for your DREAM?

_____
_____
_____
_____
_____
_____
_____
_____
_____
_____

What is your passion?

_____
_____
_____
_____
_____
_____
_____
_____
_____
_____

What are the steps you will take to pursue your dreams?

_____

_____

_____

_____

_____

_____

_____

_____

_____

_____

_____

_____

_____

Create a vision board of pictures of your dreams this year.
List some of the pictures you want to include.

_____

_____

_____

_____

_____

_____

_____

_____

Write the timeframe in which you would like to achieve your dreams;1 month, 6 months, 12months or longer.

_____

_____

_____

_____

_____

_____

_____

_____

_____

_____

_____

_____

_____

_____

_____

_____

_____

_____

_____

_____

_____

_____

About Dr. Kishma A. George

Dr. Kishma A. George can in a single phrase, be described as a Purpose Pusher. She is an inspirational speaker, mentor, playwright, producer and author. Her overarching mission is to inspire people to fulfill their God-given purpose. Dr. Kishma's work as a speaker and mentor is executed through the Women Destined for Greatness Mentoring Program in Kent County, DE. She believes that despite life's circumstances, there is greatness inside of you! Dr. Kishma A. George is the President and CEO of K.I.S.H. Home, Inc., acronym for Kingdom

Investments in Single Hearts (K.I.S.H.) K.I.S.H. Home Inc. was founded out of a desire to create a positive impact on the lives of girls and women in the state of Delaware, as well as those young women who are presently in, or who have aged out of the foster care system.

Dr. George worked as an Independent Living Mentor and witnessed the tremendous challenges foster care youth who've aged out of the system experience while trying to find their way to a self- sufficient and stable life. A passion within her grew for these young adults and their future as she experienced their frustration in handling basic skills - such as opening a checking/savings account, parenting and issues involved with single parenthood.

Dr. George knew these young adults needed a strong support system that would empower and encourage them to take control of their lives. They struggled in their transition of leaving foster care because many were still attending high school and were not emotionally or financially stable. After witnessing this, Dr. George began her journey of seeking ways to assist young adults in becoming emotionally and economically self- sufficient so that their transition from the foster care system to independent living was successful. Many of the young adults with whom she worked, left the foster care system at 18 years of age and found themselves homeless, pregnant, lacking self-esteem, incarcerated, unemployed and without guidance. As a mentor, Dr. George became frustrated by the minimum amount of resources the community offered these young adults. Dr.

Kishma opened a 24-hour transitional home for young women presently in, or who have aged out of the foster care system in Delaware. She wants to make a difference in their lives and ensure they have a safe, successful transition to independent living.

Her diligence and passion for young women have been recognized in various newspaper articles, including; the Dover Post, Delaware News Journal, Delaware State News and Milford Beacon. She was also featured in the Kingdom Voices Magazine, Gospel 4 U Magazine , K.I.S.H. Magazine , BOND Inc. and BlogSpot's weekly spotlight 'Fostered Out of Love'. In addition, she appeared as special guest on the Atlanta LIVE TV Show, Life Talk Radio Show with Coach TMB, Live TV Show Straight Talk for Women Only and The Frank and Travis Radio Show on Praise 105.1. Empowered Women Ministries have recognized Dr. Kishma as Woman of the Year in the category of Entrepreneurial Success, as well as Zeta Phi Beta Sorority, Inc. / Theta Zeta Zeta Chapter for her outstanding involvement in the Greater Dover Community. She was also presented with the Diversity Award (2013) from the State of Delaware / Social Services, the Authentic Servant Leadership Award (2014), New Castle County Chapter of the DSU Alumni Association 33rd annual Scholarship Luncheon for outstanding service to the Wilmington Community and the Delaware State University (2014), Church Girlz Rock; Humanitarian Award (2015), Faith Fighter Award (2016) , CHOICES "Woman of the Year"(2016) , State of Delaware Office of the Governor Tribute Award (2016), and Business Woman of the Year (2016).

Dr. Kishma received her Bachelor of Science degree in Psychology from Delaware State University and Honorary Doctorate of Philosophy; Humane Letters from CICA International University and Seminary. Her passion is to empower you through the Word of God and inspire you to begin living your DREAMS. No matter what your circumstances may be, God has a purpose for your life. Dr. Kishma strives to make a difference in your life and make certain that YOU will birth EVERY DREAM God has placed on the inside.

Dr. Kishma A. George is the Director of Women Destined for Greatness Mentoring Program and Visionary/Editor-in-Chief for K.I.S.H. Magazine.

To Contact Kishma A. George visit www.kishmageorge.com

Kishma's Acknowledgements

First and foremost, I want to give God all the glory and honor who made this vision possible. I love You Lord with all of my heart!

In memory of my beloved father; Edmond Felix George, I am thankful for his encouragement and inspiring me to dream.

To the best mother in the world Novita Scatliffe-George; I thank you for your love, support, encouraging words and for praying for me. Thank you for not giving up on me. I love you Mom.

To my wonderful daughter Kiniquá, I love you dearly. Thank you for your encouraging words, hugs and love.

To my family James, Raeisha, Christopher, Joshua, Seriah, Janisha and Kayla thank you for supporting the vision with your prayers and love.

A special thank you to the Co-Authors of this book. They are Romella Vaughn, Tammy Collins Markee, Marla Smith, Ayanna Moore, Danielle Ashley, Letisha Galloway, Lakisha Selby and LaKesha Logan. Thank you for sharing your story, dedication and believing in the vision.

To K.I.S.H. Home, Inc.'s Board/Advisors, Volunteers and Mentors, thank you for your dedication, support and believing in the vision in helping make a difference in the young women's lives in Delaware.

To Dr. Tracy Quintana, thank you for all your support and encouraging words.

To Pastor Ayanna, publisher, I thank God every day for bringing you into my life. You have been a blessing. Thank you for your encouraging words, support, love and believing in the vision.

Lastly, I would like to thank CTS graphics, ChosenButterfly Publishing and to everyone that encouraged, prayed, and supported K.I.S.H. Home, Inc. over the years, I am forever grateful. God bless!

About K.I.S.H. Home, Inc.

Kingdom Investments in Single Hearts (K.I.S.H.) Home, Inc. was founded in August 2008, out of the desire to make an impact in the lives of girls & women in the community as well as those young women who are presently in, or have aged out of the foster care system in Delaware. Through Ms. George's works as an Independent Living Mentor, she has mentored young adults. During her tenure as a mentor, she witnessed the tremendous challenges these young people experienced while trying to find their way to a self-sufficient and stable life.

A passion within her grew for these young adults and their future, as she experienced their frustration in handling basic skills, such as opening a checking/savings account, parenting and the frustration of single parenthood. Ms. George knew that these young adults, whether they were a single parent or single, needed a strong support system that would empower and encourage them to take control of their lives. They struggled in their transition of leaving their homes or foster care because many were still attending high school and were not emotionally or financially stable.

After witnessing this, Ms. George began her journey of seeking ways to assist young adults in becoming emotionally and economically self-sufficient so that their transition out of their homes or the foster care system and into independent living was successful. Many of the young adults with whom she worked left their homes or foster care at 18 years old, and found themselves homeless, pregnant, lacking self-esteem, incarcerated, unemployed and without guidance. As a mentor, Ms. George became frustrated by the minimum amount of resources the community offered these young adults. She wanted to make a difference in their lives and make certain that they had a safe, successful transition to adulthood and independent living.

K.I.S.H. Home, Inc. offers young women in Delaware the support they need to become emotionally stable and self-sufficient in every aspect of their lives and community.

Once again, K.I.S.H. Home, Inc. would like to thank you for the purchase of this book. Portions of the proceeds will be going to K.I.S.H. Home, Inc. a 501 (c) 3 non-profit, faith-based organization that is currently assisting the Transitional Living